To:

....

From:

....

West Side Publishing is a division of Publications International, Ltd.

Copyright © 2009 Publications International, Ltd.
All rights reserved. This book may not be reproduced or quoted in whole or
in part by any means whatsoever without written permission from:

Louis Weber, CEO
Publications International, Ltd.
7373 North Cicero Avenue
Lincolnwood, Illinois 60712

Permission is never granted for commercial purposes.

ISBN-13: 978-1-4127-1581-2
ISBN-10: 1-4127-1581-4

Manufactured in China.

8 7 6 5 4 3 2 1

Kids Say the Cutest
Things About
Dogs

Illustrations by Amanda Haley

WEST
SIDE
PUBLISHING

If you're going to love a dog, you have to be okay with getting kisses all over your face.

Montel, age 8

Dogs don't like it when you
pretend they're a pony,
even if they're big.

Kaylie, age 6

My dog's superpower is making things disappear. It's good when he makes food that I don't like disappear but bad when he makes my socks and toys disappear.

Brandon, age 7

Our dog jumped the fence
so he could be friends with
the dog next door.

Tisha, age 5

Don't play around fire hydrants. If you have a dog, you know why.

Dennis, age 8

Dogs have really bad breath. So how come they don't have to brush their teeth every night?

Manuel, age 5

I wish my dog would eat my homework. He only wants to chew on shoes.

Danny, age 8

Dogs love chasing. In movies, they chase bad guys. In real life, they chase butterflies and cats and cars.

Betsy, age 7

I'm not allowed to call my sister a dog, even though a dog is my favorite kind of animal.

Jared, age 7

My mom told me to take a catnap, but I took a dog nap instead. A dog nap is when you sprawl out on the rug in the middle of the living room and people trip over you.

Trevor, age 7

Can dogs from different countries understand each other?

Ray, age 6

Dogs are like babies, because when you take them out for walks, everyone has to stop and tell you they're cute.

Greg, age 9

Dogs never get bored. I could throw my dog a baseball for 200 years, and he would keep on fetching it. But the ball would get soggy.

Yumi, age 8

My dog wears my shoes in
his mouth.

Sandra, age 3

Mom said Dad was gonna be in the doghouse if he forgot to pick up dinner. Good thing he remembered or he would've had to sleep outside next to Mayzie!

Simaya, age 10

Dogs have a great sense of smell, but that doesn't mean they smell good.

Monica, age 8

My dog lies down when I say "sit" and runs away when I say "stay." I want to show people her tricks, but she's always playing tricks on us!

Elena, age 9

Girl dogs hate wearing dresses as much as boy dogs do.

Courtney, age 6

I love *my* dog because he keeps *me* warm all night long.

Luke, age 7

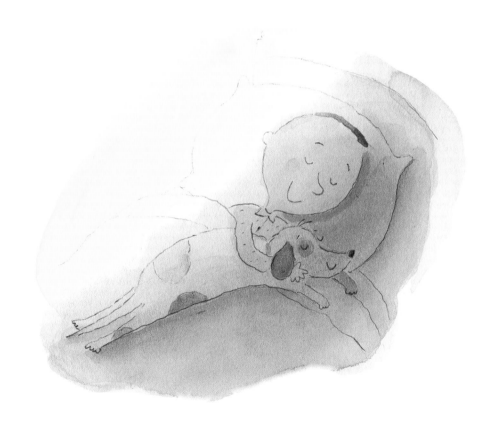

Everyone says cats are curious, but my cat's just lazy. Dogs are the ones sniffing around and discovering stuff.

Tony, age 9

My grandpa says dogs
go to dog heaven, but I
hope mine goes to people
heaven so we can play
fetch up in the clouds.

Henry, age 8

Dogs are like racecars. They go around and around and around and don't get tired. I tried it once, but I got dizzy.

Bill, age 8

We took our dog Duke to
obedience school because
the neighbor lady told my mom
that he was out of control.

Thom, age 8

Don't make your tree house your clubhouse, 'cause your dog won't be able to join.

Max, age 7

Our dog is always barking at stuff we can't see. I think he has secret powers.

Kelly, age 5

My teacher said we have to do our book reports on our own, but my dog decided to finish mine.

Ellen, age 10

Dogs are good best friends
to have, because if your
family moves, you get to bring
your best friend with you.

Rachel, age 9

No matter how much cat food you give him, a dog won't meow.

Nelson, age 9

I want a puppy, but Mom
says that she already
cleans up enough after
Daddy.

Samantha, age 7

Dogs chase cats because cats annoy them. That's why I chase my little sister.

Peyton, age 9

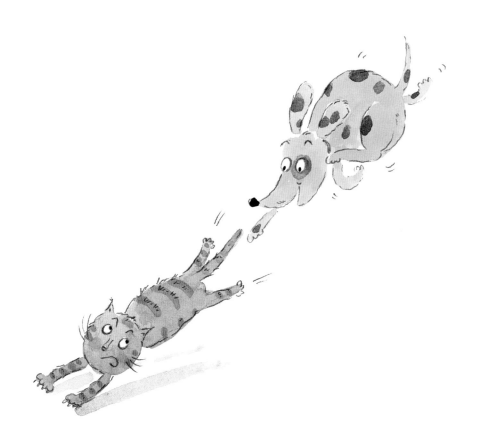

My dog loves broccoli,
which is great because
I hate it.

Carrie, age 7

Dogs are the softest pillows for when you're watching TV.

Lyra, age 7

People say dogs have clean mouths, but I don't think so. Have you seen what my dog eats?

Janelle, age 10

A dog will do almost
anything for a treat, like
sit, stay, or roll over. I wish
I got dessert that easy.

Gretchen, age 9

My dog barks at the vacuum cleaner. He thinks it's barking back.

Waylon, age 9

Dogs are called "Man's Best Friend," because when you have a dog, you don't get sad.

Austin, age 4

Amanda Haley graduated from The School of the Art Institute of Chicago with a BFA in painting and drawing. She has illustrated more than 40 children's books, including both fictional and educational titles. Haley lives in Virginia with her husband, Brian, and dog, Mayzie.

Publications International, Ltd., wishes to thank the following schools for their submissions to *Kids Say the Cutest Things About Dogs*:
Brennermann School (Chicago, IL), Bush Elementary School (Fulton, MO), Conn–West Elementary School (Grandview, MO), Gilkey Elementary School (Plainwell, MI), Holy Family School (Granite City, IL), Kennedy Middle School (Kankakee, IL), King Lab Magnet School (Evanston, IL), Plantation Park Elementary School (Plantation, FL), St. Agatha Catholic Academy (Chicago, IL), Starr Elementary School (Plainwell, MI)